# A STORYBOOK FOR ADULTS AND OTHER CHILDREN

## For Mental Health Professionals, Teachers and Families

Jerri Curry, Ph.D., LMFT, CAODC

Paperback: ISBN: 978-0-578-46611-8
Ebook: 978-0-578-46612-5

Historical: 0-944586-00-7

Book Design: Ghislain Viau, Creative Publishing Book Design (2019)
Book Design:  Susan Pinkerton, The Swan (1988)
Illustrations by Sarah Poppler (1987)
Audio:  Studio Z Recording, Inc. The Swan (1988)
Video: David Ronan, Crushpix.com (2019)

Library of Congress Cataloging in Publication data
Main entry under title:
A Storybook for Adults and Other Children

Printed in the United States of America

This book is dedicated to the mental health professionals, teachers and parents who place clients and children first and who have dedicated their lives to helping raise collective, compassionate consciousness in the community and children of all ages.

With my deepest appreciation for some very special people who provided support, talent and wisdom in the final creation of A Storybook for Adults and Other Children. My friends, colleagues and professionals who assisted in the audio portion of this project are Sharon Robinson, Mark Hanson, Pat Okerson, Jennie Romero, Hugh Thomas, Elle Boone, Alyson Steel and James Seawell. Thank you.

# TABLE OF CONTENTS

# THE SWAN
## (Theme: Connection and Separation)

**CHORUS**

The pond began to ripple from the center toward the shore. The cattails swayed gently in the breeze while the swans began to ascend in flight. As they took off in unison, the pond residents watched the spread of their magnificent wings as they soared toward the heavens.

**DOVE**

They show such beauty; such elegant grace.
Those snow white birds
Flying together at a perfect pace.

**CHORUS**

Said the little dove with the angelic face.

**LITTLE FROG**

Look at that one flying alone.
That is strange for swans always have a mate.
I wonder what caused her special fate?

**CHORUS**

Mrs. Frog asked the residents of Puddle Pond

## MOTHER FROG

That is a strange sight indeed,
What has caused her to be alone?
Was she that way when she made the pond her home?

## THOMAS the TOAD

As I think back, it seems to me,
there was a swan who was single and fancy-free.
The story I remember was a tender one indeed.
Come gather around and I will proceed.

## CHORUS

Thomas the toad said as he puffed on his pipe.
The Puddle Pond residents swam quickly to shore. No one wanted to
miss what Thomas had in store.

## GUPPY FISH

Tell us, Thomas, about the swan who lived alone.
What she was like when Puddle Pond was her home?

## CHORUS

The guppy fish said as they swam toward the surface of the water.

## THOMAS the TOAD

Oh what a beauty! Crystal was her name.
For she sparkled like snow drops glistening on a window pane.
No one compared to her in elegance and style.
Where ever she went, others would nod and smile.
Even as a tiny swan she would glide on the pond.
Lifting her wings creating a breeze in song.
She was a gentle swan who shared her soul.
She would sit for hours telling stories,
to the young and old.
She would make them laugh,
And sometimes they would cry;
But not out of sadness; that wasn't the reason why.
The story would just touch each heart,
And the listener's tears would fall from the start.
She would make up the stories as she went along;
Reaching deep within herself,
Looking for a moral to help teach others to be strong.
The Puddle Pond citizens loved her very much.
Her white feathers so soft to the touch.

## CHORUS

Thomas quietly said as he continued to puff on his pipe.

## BUCKY BEAVER

Well, what happened to Crystal?
What made her be alone?
And why did she decide to leave this lovely home?

## CHORUS

Bucky Beaver asked with some bewilderment.

## THOMAS the TOAD

Many years ago, Puddle Pond was a very busy place.
With birds flying in, calling this their base.
They would gather here during summer time —
Feeding, swimming and mates they would find.
It was a time well spent—
The birds were happy; they seemed content.
And then one summer, a new swan appeared.
He swooped down toward the pond just about here.

## THOMAS the TOAD

He was a regal sort of chap
With his head held high.
He glanced around the pond
And it was then that he spied.
Crystal gliding near the south end of the shore.
He had never seen such a beauty before.
He hesitated before moving too fast.
She looked so fragile in the water that shimmered like glass.
For the longest time, he stayed very still,
Just admiring her gave him a chill.
She was certainly one of a kind
He knew another like this he would never find.
Crystal continued to glide along the shore.
Seemingly content without wanting more.
But then she looked toward his way.
And stared for what seemed like a day.

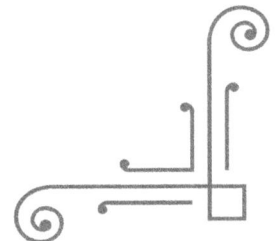

He began to move toward her with shyness it seemed.
And she did the same, as if in a dream.
Their glide was like music as they danced on the pond,
Around one another, they began to respond.
As they reached out, their wings brushed by,
And then he noticed a tear in her eye.
He touched her gently asking her why.
And all she could do was continue to cry.
Finally, she stopped and looked up at him.
Being alone for so long made her have fear,

But now that was gone, having him here.
Her tears came from knowing this was right,
and so together they held one another
through the warm, summer night.

The days moved along at a very slow pace
Puddle Pond now had become a more special place.
Crystal thrived and grew with such grace.
Her beautiful eyes glowed in her very soft face.
He showered her with rose petals,
And sprinkled daisies on her back.
While she made sure there was nothing he lacked.
She sang quiet songs and told him stories from her heart.
They both knew that the commitment they made
meant they would never part.

Their word was their bond.
This commitment came from their soul.
First as individuals and then together they would become whole.
The years went by, and the happiness they shared
continued to reinforce how much they each cared.
They had many fine days, and many good years.
There was much joy and laughter—very few tears.

And as they grew old,
They knew their time was coming to an end,
and it happened one day, beginning with him.
She held him in her wings as he looked in her face.
He was remembering her loving and gentle grace.
Slowly he drifted, as she held him close by,
and then a tear dropped from her eye.
Crystal then began to swim toward the center of the pond,
For, she too was remembering the days long ago.
When life with him had helped her to grow.

She remembered the commitment they had made,
And how he had helped her stop being afraid.
He had eased her fears. He taught her to trust.
He had been a good partner, fair and just.
She knew she would never forget his loving touch.
And so, she quietly swam near the Weeping Willow tree,
waiting to join him and finally be free.
The day has come, my Puddle Pond friends.
This is the day when for Crystal, it finally will end.

Her time of waiting has come to a close.
She is flying to meet the one she long ago chose.
You see, for Crystal, commitment came from her soul,
and it is only through herself, and the universe,
and in partnership she would become whole.

# The Swan
## Connection and Separation

As a young swan, Crystal spends the beginning of her life with other residents of Puddle Pond sharing stories and laughter. Life is serene, and she is perfectly content. One day a new Swan appears and, while responding to one another, Crystal learns to share the deepest part of herself. She and her partner express feelings of love and their willingness to honor the relationship through commitment.

# The Swan
## Story Guide

1.  In the story, Crystal was content before she met the Swan. The story talks about Crystal becoming whole as an individual and through the Universe, and then through partnership she will be whole. What does whole mean?

2.  Crystal and the Swan fell in love in Puddle Pond. Crystal and her partner were in love, and they also loved one another. How would they explain the difference between being in love and loving someone?

3.  Crystal and her partner made a commitment for life. What did the word commitment mean to Crystal? What did it mean to her partner? Do you think Crystal and her partner found it difficult to remain committed for a whole lifetime to each other? What are some things that could have made one of them want to break the commitment?

4.  Crystal and her partner had some good times together. What fun things did they do during their time together? What might have been some difficult times not mentioned in the story?

5.  What Crystal and her partner realized that their time was coming to an end, what feelings might they have experienced (sad, angry, anxious, confused, guilty, relieved)? What kind of fears might they feel about death? Would it have been helpful for them to talk about their fears?

# Reflections

6. The Puddle Pond residents loved Crystal very much. Draw a picture, with crayons or paints, that describe the feeling of love. Use the word love and connect the picture to that word through your art. Use colors that describe the word love.

7. Pick out one of the other animals in Puddle Pond and make up a story about that animal. Write or tell the story to other members of your family or a group of friends. What are you trying to teach others?

8. Crystal and her partner loved each other very much. Write a letter to those you love telling them what it is you love the most about each of them. You might decide to mail the letters.

9. Put on a record without lyrics. Lie down and close your eyes. Picture yourself as a leaf on Puddle Pond. While you listen to the music, imagine floating on the pond like Crystal. Turn the leaf into anything that you want it to be and then begin a guided fantasy of your own until the music is over.

10. Crystal had very positive stories to tell the residents of Puddle Pond. Positive stories and statements can be very helpful in solving personal problems. Create a positive statement for yourself that will help you. Example: My relationships make me happy, healthy, wealthy and wise. Write and say out loud a similar positive statement ten times each day for twenty days and see if there is a difference in the way you feel at the end of that twenty days.

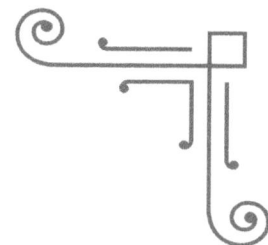

# PUFFER
## (Theme: Friendship)

**CHORUS**

Clear skies, mountains and valley with clouds beginning to form. Some clouds are big, dark and billowy. Others are small and wispy. Each cloud has its' own personality and shape. Each is different. Puffer's mother and her friend Windy urge Puffer to join them and fly off together. The clouds leave while Puffer remains sitting above a tall mountain with a little Redwood tree sitting beneath Puffer on the mountain top. Days passed and other clouds would move through, look at Puffer and keep moving along.

**PUFFER**

Well you really are small, little one.
How long have you been down there away from the sun?
You look wet and tired, little tree.
Why do you sit right under me?

**LITTLE REDWOOD TREE**

I want a chance to begin to grow,
But with you always there it's hard you know.
I'm little and I want to grow strong.
But I can't if you don't go where you belong.
I need the sunshine and I need your shade,
But without any sunshine I will soon fade!
I'm all wet because I've been crying.
Sitting here each day; trying and trying,
To grow in spite of you up there.
I wonder, sometimes, if you even care.

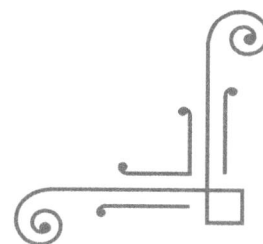

## PUFFER

Oh goodness I had no idea you were so sad.
I hope you don't think I've been intentionally bad.
My friends had wanted me to travel with them.
To just pick up with the next gust of wind.
But I was afraid to leave my favorite spot
on this majestic mountain top.
I know, why don't I just move an inch or two,
And then maybe some growth will come to you?

## LITTLE REDWOOD TREE

Why are you so afraid, Puffer?
Clouds are supposed to move and see the world.
But you stay here like a frightened little girl.
My roots go in to the ground,
And I can't easily move around.

Why don't you take off and have some fun?
If, like you, we could fly through the sky,
We wouldn't sit around and ask why.
You would not catch us here.
Simply because of fear.

Take off and see all there is to see.
Learn and grow and be all you can be.
When you grow old, and have had a full life.
Return and share with us, your many insights.

## PUFFER

I don't know where I will go or who I will see.
But you are right in telling me.
To grow and be all that I can be.
Take care, my friend, the little tree.
Thank you for your wisdom and concern.
I'm ready to travel now and see what I can learn.

## CHORUS

Puffer gathers up her wispy body and floats through the blue sky. Initially, she moves slowly and cautiously, but soon gains confidence and begins to move faster and faster toward the distant skies as she glances back at the tree who had become her friend.

## LITTLE REDWOOD TREE

The best of luck Puffer. Have a wonderful time.
See the world. I know you'll do just fine.
Life will turn out to be good for you.
You'll have many experiences.
Certainly, more than just a few.

## CHORUS

Puffer flew by day and she flew by night.
Strangest of all, she felt no fright.
Puffer saw the blue oceans.
With their waves going in and out,
and she saw the great whale,
With water coming from its spout.
The South Sea Islands were sights to behold.
Dotted with palm trees in a land never cold.
She saw children running along the beach,

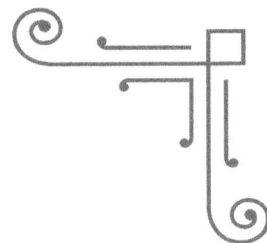

And she provided them shade from the sun's steady heat.
She saw castles on hillsides and animals in the field.
She knew she could give protection and shield.
She came to the great pyramids that stood high in the sky.
and she learned they were built before she could fly.

She saw the endless motion of time.
Reaching across the desert sand.
In a harsh but yet pure and distant land.
She touched the beauty of the desert flower,
and framed the awesome desert sunset with a rainbow of shower.

Statues stood tall and proud.
As Puffer enfolded them in a mist like shroud.
Faces of men sat on a mountainside.
Puffer was so startled she thought she would collide.
She found herself traveling along a great wall,
Wondering when it would end or would it ever fall?

She saw the stars come out at night.
And the twinkle of their magic was a glorious sight.
The waterfalls and forests grew over the land.
Puffer saw a world she thought was truly grand.

The icicles hung from the window panes,
And the snowflakes fell like spun sugar rain.
Towns were covered with the witness of snow.
And often the Old North Wind would blow.
But that didn't bother Puffer at all.
The Old Wind just helped her change shape and grow tall.
It was a day late in Spring.
When Puffer saw what seemed like an incredible dream.

Puffer had been traveling with a few friends.
Watching rainbows with pots of gold at the end.

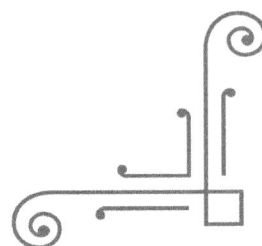

When all of a sudden, her mother and Windy, she spied.
They rushed toward each other and began to cry.
The tears fell to the ground for many a day.
There was so much talking; so much to say.
They wrapped their loving arms around each other,
And the clouds gathered to smother,
Each other with soggy, wet kisses,
And the most embracing warm wishes.

They had much to catch up on', and began telling tales.
How much they had learned about pyramids and whales.
Once they had finished, the clouds moved through the air.
Racing toward mountain tops with dramatic flair.
The older and wiser clouds showed the way,
And Puffer found herself on an exciting journey each day.
They moved through mountains and towns,
And along the roads where many sights were found.
For years they traveled, gathering together for storms.
Often, they sent Puffer ahead so the people were warned.
The crops welcomed the coming clouds.
The people cheered for the coming rain,
And Puffer learned about friendships.
Never again would she be the same.

Some Indian tribes celebrated through the night;
they danced and sang rain songs by the fire light.
The rivers glowed with a new Spring water,
And the dams were built by the river otter.
Leaves traveled down the gentle streams,
And Puffer knew the Earth had been cleaned.

As years went by, Puffer grew old.
With the coming winter, she began to feel cold.
She had lived life to the fullest,

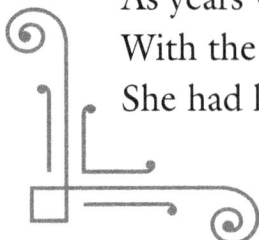

And she was grateful she could blend.
She had traveled the world.
And now it was time for it to end.

She remembered her friend from the mountain top.
There she would return for her final stop.
The tiny tree who had touched her with his cry,
She now understood the reason why.

She told the clouds to learn and always grow.
That was the way to understand life and to know.
Nothing was more important than being a friend,
Giving love and having a helping hand to extend.

With that message she leaped through the sky.
And in an instant, she was at the mountain high and dry.
She looked for her friend, the little tree.
who had given her such wise advice.
She wanted to thank him for helping her.
To ponder carefully and to think twice.
But the tiny tree seemed to be nowhere around,
And Puffer's tears began to fall to the ground.
All of a sudden, Puffer cried,

**PUFFER**

My goodness! I don't believe what I see,
you've become a gigantic redwood tree.

**GROWN REDWOOD TREE**

It's true I am no longer small.
My branches stick out and I am very tall.
You too have changed Puffer, my friend.
Tell me what it was like,
Under the rainbow, and at Earth's end?

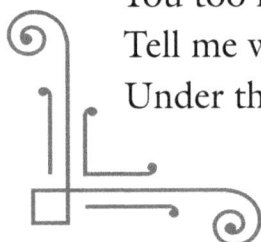

## PUFFER

It is a land of magic with friendships of all kinds,
And my journey lasted more than a life time.
Thank you for helping me see the Light,
Let's talk about my journey through the night.
I will wrap myself around you, gigantic redwood tree.
Let us melt together and forever one we will be.

# Puffer
## Friendship

Puffer is content to float above her favorite spot on a mountain top. She watches the other clouds take off for new sights but Puffer does not go with them. A little tree befriends Puffer and through their conversations, Puffer realizes that she needs to learn more about life and the importance of friends. Puffer travels throughout the world and after she grows old, she returns to share her experiences with the little tree who had become her friend long ago.

# Puffer
## Story Guide

1. Why do you think Puffer was so afraid? Have you ever felt afraid to meet other people? What would you do to stop being afraid? Is there anything that you are afraid of now? Describe that fear to a trusted individual. Explore ways that you can overcome that fear.

2. What was her friend the little tree trying to teach Puffer? Take a trip with your family or friends and look for your own special tree. Touch the tree and try to feel it talk to you. What might your tree teach you?

3. What did Puffer and her friends teach you that you didn't know before about friendships? List five ways in which you could be a better friend to someone. Follow up on one of these ways with a person you would like to be better friends with in the future.

4. While traveling Puffer saw many sights. Try to name as many of the sights as you can. Example: The faces in the mountainside is called Mount Rushmore in the United States.

5. What happened when Puffer and her mother and Windy found each other. What happened to the ground?

## Reflections

6. What does friendship mean to you? Who is your best friend? Can you give that friend a big hug right now or the next time you are together? Tell your friend something you learned today. Have your friend do the same.

7. Are there any places you would like to visit if you were Puffer? Name five and tell why you would like to see these particular places. Go to a travel agency and get brochures of these places. Make a wish that you will have the opportunity to visit these places.

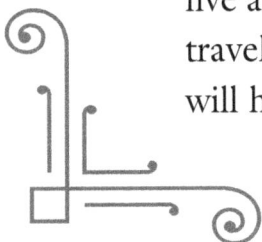

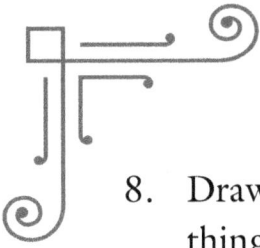

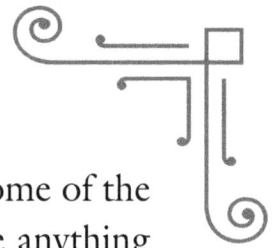

8. Draw a picture of your very own Puffer. Be sure to draw some of the things Puffer saw in her travels around the world. Is there anything new you would have Puffer see that wasn't in the story?

9. Close your eyes and have a family member or friend take you on a special guided imagery. The family member or friend can guide you through a journey that you can see in your mind. When you get through, share the trip out loud.

10. Paint a picture of your favorite place. Example: Puffer was on a mountain top overlooking the trees. Tell your family or friends why this is your favorite spot.

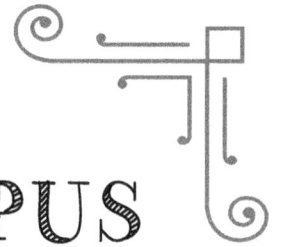

# OLD OLLIE THE OCTOPUS

## (Theme: Fear)

**CHORUS**

Deep in the ocean, on the rocky floor, amid dark caves and dense seaweed the bustling community of sea creatures scurried about, swimming, and chasing one another in a playful scene. Ollie was sitting on the top of a round, black rock and watching the others playing and swimming.

Ollie wishes he could join in the fun with the other sea creatures but his parents forbade him from leaving the rock. They warned him of great storms that blew, of sea monsters that sprang from dark places, of earthquakes that opened cracks in the floor through which he might fall never to be seen again. As Ollie hears these frightening stories, he clung even tighter, and his parents smiled because they knew Ollie would stay safe.

**MOTHER OCTOPUS**

Sweet little Ollie, don't be afraid my dear,
Your father and I must go and leave you here.
We'll be hunting for lunch down by the dock.
Be a good boy and stay on your favorite rock.

**CHORUS**

Of course, Ollie obediently would sit on this seat.
And he wondered what his mother would bring him to eat.

**OLD OLLIE the OCTOPUS**

Perhaps mom will bring me a lobster or two.
Perhaps they will capture more than a few.
Out by the dock there are all kinds of fish.
I bet they bring me a tasty dish.

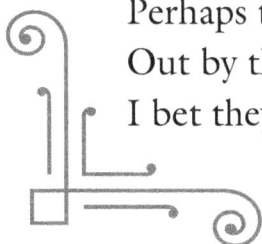

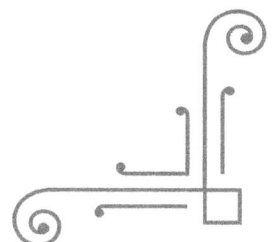

**CHORUS**

Lunchtime came and went. The afternoon passed. Ollie's stomach growled with hungry. Suppertime came and still no mom and dad. The sun went down. The other sea creatures journeyed home and Ollie wondered if his parents got lost. Ollie continued to wait night and day. He imagined fierce sea monsters and earthquakes and turbulent storms so he stayed clasped tightly to his rock; not daring to leave this spot. On the second morning after his parents' disappearance, Uncle Squid found Ollie sitting and suffering silently. Holding his hat in his hand, he said:

**UNCLE SQUID**

I'm afraid that I bring you some very bad news.
I would have another tell you if I could choose.

**CHORUS**

Ollie looked at Uncle Squid, prepared for a shock as he clutched his rock.

**OLD OLLIE the OCTOPUS**

Go on!

**UNCLE SQUID**

Your folks have been caught in a fisherman's sack.
Take courage, dear Ollie, they won't be coming back.

**CHORUS**

Ollie realized what Uncle Squid was saying.
He would now give up his constant praying.
His parents were gone and he was all alone.
The big, black rock would forever be his home.

He was too afraid to ever think of leaving this place.
He would stay forever because of fears he could not face.
Many years passed and Ollie became older and less bolder.
Sometimes he would think of changing his mind,
but then he would be gripped by terror,
And afraid he would commit an awful error.
So, he stayed where he was, alone in his fears.
He was called "Old" Ollie with the passing years.

One day a sawfish heard about this strange octopus who had refused to leave his rock. Sammy the Sawfish decided it was time to do something about this unusual situation.

## SAMMY the SAWFISH

"Goodness sakes, I can't believe what I see,
You need someone to help you be free.
Now don't worry, my saw won't get too close.
I will saw and saw some more,
Until you are free from this ocean floor.
If I saw too close, just nudge me with your head.
I'll stop, and find another way, instead.

## OLD OLLIE the OCTOPUS

Don't be silly. I don't want to leave my favorite rock.
Leave me alone. Go saw on a fishing dock.

## SAMMY the SAWFISH

You don't want to leave your rock?
My goodness that puts me in a state of shock.

## OLD OLLIE the OCTOPUS

There isn't a thing I want to see.
So, go away and just let me be.

## SAMMY the SAWFISH

Well, if you just want to sit, be my guest.
I'm off to the Caribbean for a long summer rest.

## CHORUS

Days later, a red snapper by the name of Happer sees Ollie.

## HAPPER the SNAPPER

This is indeed a strange sight.
I think I'll wander over and have a bite.

## OLD OLLIE the OCTOPUS

Ouch, go away! You have no business biting me.
I'm a live octopus, can't you see?

## HAPPER the SNAPPER

Oh goodness, you are alive.
You were just sitting with a stare.
Why don't you move? Don't you care?

## OLD OLLIE the OCTOPUS

Please go away.
You haven't been invited to stay.
Leave me alone.
This isn't your home.
I don't need to move around.
I am firmly planted on this rock in the ground.
It takes a lot of work to sit here, holding tight.

You guys think I'm lazy and not very bright.
But it takes time and work.
I have responsibilities I cannot shirk.
I watch the tides move in and out.
And wonder when my dinner will come about?
Seaweed settles on the ocean floor
And I have problems, problems galore.
Its' leaves tangle around me.
Pulling and tugging, winding around my rock.
I don't think it will ever stop.
I have enough worries,
I don't need more.
So, swim off to a distant shore.

## CHORUS

A few days later, a jellyfish wanders by Ollie.

## JUDY JELLYFISH

I've been traveling day and night.
Since I heard about your plight.
Everyone said that an Old Octopus by the name of Ollie.
Won't leave his spot on a big, black rock.
I didn't believe it, but by golly they were right,
You are a sad sight!

## OLD OLLIE the OCTOPUS

You need not be sad for I'm just fine.
If you just left, I'd consider the gesture kind.
Don't look at me as if I were some sideshow attraction.
You visitors are leading me to distraction.
I just want to be left alone,
So please, little Jellyfish, head for home.

## JUDY JELLYFISH

Well, I won't stay where I am not treated nice.
And others won't want to come and they will think twice.
About a visit with someone so rude,
I'm going to tell them you are in a lousy mood.

## CHORUS

Day after day, Old Ollie sat on his rock.
And day after day, no one stopped to talk.
Old Ollie wondered if he had said too much,
Now with the other fish he was out of touch.
He saw a school of fish swim by,
And he wished he could and said "should I try?"
But Ollie chose not to change
He decided his life he would not rearrange.

## OLD OLLIE the OCTOPUS

I wonder what they learn in their school.
Or if they grow up to just be a fool?
I can sit here and think as I please.
When my lunch comes by, I'll give it a squeeze.
Who cares if my friends don't come by any more.

I'll sit on my rock here on the ocean floor.

## CHORUS

The ocean would calm during a summer day.
And baby fishes would be hatched in the bay.
But when winter storms came to Ollie's place.
The waves would batter his body and face.
The water would splash up against his rock,
And leave Ollie tattered and in shock.
Old Ollie could have found shelter in a dark cave.
But that would be no way to behave.

He remembered his parents' number one rule.
To keep him from venturing in a world so cruel,
No, he must be content with his life,
Even though pressured by constant strife.

Tossing and turning, hitting and churning,
Old Ollie was battered each day.
The storms were violent, bruising and beating Ollie every which way.

## EARL the ELECTRIC EEL

I have come to help you, though you would never ask.
You're so proud, but you need help with this task.
You can't stay in this storm or you'll be hurt.
When I give the word, I'll zap you and you can fall to the dirt.
Electric eels have special power.
Stand by and with electricity, I will shower.
In one moment, you will be free.
Then you can swim over and thank me.

## OLD OLLIE the OCTOPUS

I don't want to be zapped by sparks!
Go find a big hole and hide in the dark.
If I wanted your help, I'm not too proud,
I would have yelled right out loud!

## CHORUS

Old Ollie went back to holding ever so tight.
for the storm raged on, day and night.

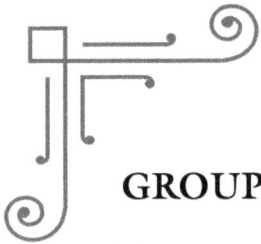

## GROUPIE FISH

We came because we want to help.
How did you get caught up in all that kelp?
We can shift your old body.
Okay, guys let's heave ho,
With one big shove we can start this show.
Reach around the back and slip under his skin,
We can do it! Let's begin!
That's the secret to our success,
Working together, we do our best.

## OLD OLLIE the OCTOPUS

How long will it take,
For everyone to learn I have a lot at stake?
Sure, this wasn't the best way to live,
But I didn't think I had much to give.
I never thought about learning more,
Even though life had a lot in store
This is my home. This is my rock.
Please go away and take your flock.

## CHORUS

As the groupie fish swim off, the needle fish approach Ollie and try to comfort him

## NEEDLE FISH

Your cuts and scrapes need to mend.
Won't you let us help you friend?
We won't try to convince you to leave this place.
We can see you're frightened by the look on your face.
So, stay here for the rest of your years,
At the end of your life you can face your fears.

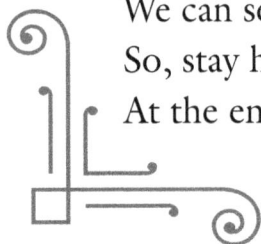

## OLD OLLIE the OCTOPUS

Fear has always kept me here;
I held my parents' advice so near.
I never learned to share.
I never learned what it was to care.
Now, it's too late. I just watch the world go by,
Yes, its' much too late to even cry.

## CHORUS

Old Ollie knew he could not leave his home.
During the storms he had been tempted to roam,
But now it was too late.
This would be forever his fate.
He had grown old and would have to stay.
And make the best of it, day after day.

## ANGEL FISH

Old Ollie, Old Ollie, you don't understand.
If you finally let go,
and follow the flow.
You will become a part of the Master Plan.

## CHORUS

Ollie looks around and sees a delicate dish,
She is the very pretty little Angel fish.
Everyone had heard of her,
She spoke to Ollie out of love and concern.
The Angelfish wanted Ollie to learn.
To trust himself and follow the flow,
And he could only do this by letting go.
As the angelfish begins to swim away,
she hears him saying.

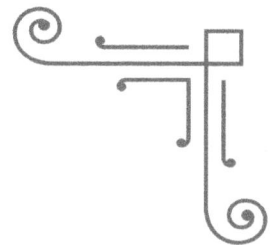

## OLD OLLIE the OCTOPUS

For the second time in my life, I'm crying.
I've spent years just trying.
To maintain control by not moving ahead,
And all that has gotten me is here instead.
I now understand what the Angelfish said so sweetly,
I know what I've been missing so completely.
I must accept that life has some pain,
If I am to learn and love I am to gain.
I must trust others,
And most of all, I must trust me.
If I am to have peace and finally be free.
If we hide our heads, we learn only fear,
And that's no reason for being here.
My life has been less than complete.
By changing my ways some new friends, I may meet,
It's never too late to change and grow,
By trusting myself, I'll gain the knowledge to know.
By choosing to finally let go,
I'll be able to follow the flow.
Now I more fully understand,
I, too, am part of the Master Plan.

# Old Ollie the Octopus
## Fear

When Ollie was just a small Octopus his parents told him not to leave his rock because of sea monsters that could hurt him. Ollie spends his life sitting on top of his rock out of fear of being harmed. The sea animals try to get Ollie off his rock, but he won't budge. Finally, the Angelfish tells Ollie that by letting go he is learning to trust the natural flow and ultimately learning to trust in himself.

# Old Ollie the Octopus
## Story Guide

1. Take a trip to the aquarium and see if you can find an Octopus. Take paper and crayons with you so you can draw a picture of the Octopus. Give your Octopus a special name.

2. Why do you think Mr. and Mrs. Octopi made Ollie stay on the rock? Were those good reasons for staying on the rock? If you were Ollie's parent what would you have told him to do?

3. How did Ollie feel when his parents disappeared? What would you have done if you had been Ollie? Have you ever been lost? What did it feel like? What did you do to find your way?

4. Name all the different types of fish that tried to help Ollie get off his rock? Who do you think was the friendliest? Who was not?

5. What do you think the Angelfish meant by suggesting to Ollie that he follow the flow? What is a master plan? Discuss your answers with your family or friends.

## Reflections

6. Think about having a fish tank with fishes in it. If you have others living with you, you will need to get their opinions before buying the fish tank and fishes.

7. Read a book about fish. List all the different kinds of fish there are in the ocean. Name something special about each fish that you list. What type of fish would you like to be? Why?

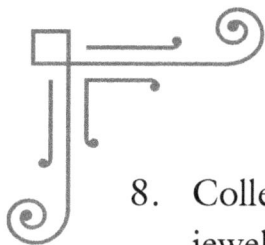

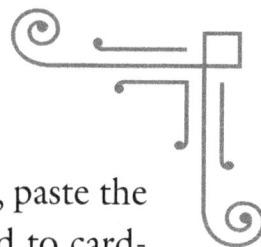

8. Collect old costume jewelry. When you have collected a lot, paste the jewelry into a fish or fishes on to a blue velvet cloth stapled to cardboard. Then get a frame so you can have a pretty picture to keep or give as a present.

9. What do you think Ollie was really afraid of besides Sea monsters and earthquakes? What are you the most afraid of? Make a list of all your fears. Then make a list on how you can overcome each of those fears.

10. Pretend you are Ollie sitting on a rock. Have your family or friends take turns being Ollie. Try to talk each other off the rock. How do you feel about what they are saying? Can you be convinced to leave the rock? Talk about the role-playing experience with each other.

# SNOWFLAKE
## (Theme: Being in the Moment)

**CHORUS**

Snowflake had to decide fast or she'd be left behind. None of the others agonized over choosing but Snowflake wasn't like the others. She carefully considered everything in her life. No one told her to decide, but she felt she had to. Ever since she was a tiny glistening speck of water, Snowflake knew that one day she'd have to make this decision. It wasn't easy being a snowflake and wondering where to land.

Earth was big and beautiful. Landing in just the right spot was very important, especially if you were a tiny snowflake. Where she landed would affect the world. She couldn't take that lightly. So Snowflake thought, and thought some more, She needed help. Of course! The Heavenly Gate Library. It had so many books. She pulled herself together and whisked off toward the large, magnificent brick building sitting on the hilltop overlooking the City of Heavenly Gate. Snowflake almost tumbled over Sammy the Snowman waddling down the street.

**SAMMY SNOWMAN**

Hello, Snowflake, how are you this bright and shiny day?
Hey, slow down, my friend and don't run away".

**SNOWFLAKE**

Oh, I'm going to the library to read as much as I can.
I have to study, and learn about man.
Soon I'll be falling to Planet Earth.
It's a duty I have and one I won't shirk.

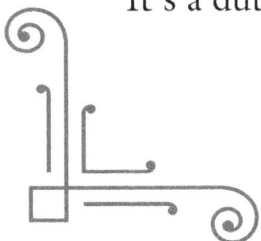

## SAMMY SNOWMAN

Well, that sounds like quite a task.
And what is the answer you're looking for, if I might ask?

## SNOWFLAKE

It may not be easy, but I'm going to try,
I must know the best place to land and why.
I'll read everything and that will take time,
But when I'm through, I'll have a fine mind.
In order to have the greatest impact.
I'll gather a lot of information and learn every fact.
When I learn all I need to know.
I can drop down to Earth, down there below.
People will stop and really look,
Maybe I'll be listed in a famous book.
So now I must go or I will be late.
I certainly don't want to miss my special fate.

## CHORUS

Snowflake rushed by Sammy Snowman and raced passed other citizens of
Heavenly Gate and entered the library.

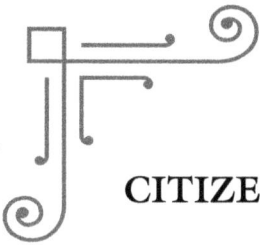

## CITIZENS OF HEAVENLY GATE

Where is she going in such a big hurry?
And why does she have such a look of worry?

## SNOWFLAKE

Hi, I'm here to read every book about the Earth below.
Bring out all you have before I go.

I want to know about the Winter season.
I will try to read every book within reason.
Show me the highest mountain in the land,
And tell me about snow in the city and the desert sand.
Is any famous statute more famous than the rest?
I must have this information to pass my greatest test.

Give me something that will help me,
So that I can be...
The most famous Snowflake of all.
Everyone must notice when I finally fall.

This book says the Earth is pleasant and green.
In this book there are many beautiful scenes.
I could land on the biggest mountain of all,
But no one would notice because it is so tall.
I could drift on to a tiny winter flower,
Or be the first snowflake in an icy shower.

Where should I land?
How about the desert sand?
But there's little snow in a desert,
So that won't work at all,
What a terrible thing, not knowing where to fall!

In this book I see a statute of a man.
Perhaps if I fell on his upturned hand,
People would see,
And all would point at famous little me.
No, not there, they'd be looking at him.
I'd be lost, another speck in the wind.
I'm getting tired of reading these books.
How am I to decide. Where am I to look?

**CHORUS**

Nearby, Ozzie the Wise Old Owl sits on a little stool in the corner of
the library.
He leans over and whispers to Snowflake.

**OZZIE THE WISE OLD OWL**

Go see the fair lady in the Snow Palace near the Lake.
She can tell you how to become famous.
She knows the answer to your final fate.

## SNOWFLAKE

The Snow Princess is exactly who I will see,
Your suggestion is great! Now, please excuse me!
I'll just whisk through a window and find the throne,
I wonder if she's even at home?
My, such a cold place and so full of frost,
I hope I don't get lost.
Oh, that must be the Lady Fair,
How beautiful she is with that golden hair.
I have come to ask your advice on an important matter.
Please excuse my mumbling but it's so cold,
and my teeth are beginning to chatter.

## SNOW PRINCESS

I felt your presence in the hall.
What can I do? Why have you come to call?

## SNOWFLAKE

I have to decide where to land.
I want to make a spectacular last stand.
Snowflakes are treated all alike,
but I want to be different from the rest.
Can you tell me which landing place would be the best?

## SNOW PRINCESS

You place great importance on being so rare.
Why do you want people to stare?
Remember, the goal you reach only has merit,
If you enjoy each day and learn to share it.
Having impact is an important quest,
But learning to just live each moment is a greater test.
Living in each moment is not always easy to do.
But it is what life is about, so Snowflake it is up to you.

## SNOWFLAKE

Thank you, Snow Princess, for your wise advice.
You're right and I don't have to think twice.

## CHORUS

As Snowflake returns home, she begins to realize,
How important just falling can be.
Before learning that, she had not been free.
She was so worried about being seen.
She had forgotten about the moments in between,
The trip itself would be the best part of all,
With her newfound knowledge, she got ready for the fall.
She polished her little crystals as bright as could be,
And shaped up her points for all to see.
While falling to Earth, she would have fun,
And wherever she landed, she'd sparkle in the sun.

## CHORUS

As Snowflake whistled cheerfully, the other snowflakes ran to her asking…

## OTHER SNOWFLAKES

Where have you decided to land?
Where will be your final stand?

## SNOWFLAKE

You know, I have thought about this fall,
And now I'm not worried at all.
Why who knows? I may be caught in the wind,
And land with any of you, dear friends.
I think I will let myself just go
And not worry about the final show.
Some things should be left to fate.
Planning in advance would be a mistake.
So, as we fall, both during the day and at night,
Lets' enjoy every moment, looking at each sight.
And if you see a place that you like,
Then go to that spot and land in a twinkle,
Everywhere the landscape will be sprinkled.
You might choose the tip of a reindeer's nose,
Or perhaps a porch light at night as it glows.
A child may be playing outside for an hour,
And you may touch his hand during our shower.

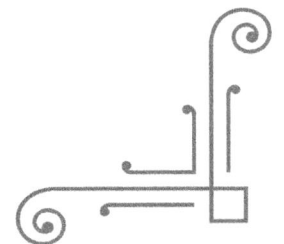

You may float down on a frozen lake,
To help strengthen the water so people can skate.
Land wherever you choose,
With this wonderful Earth, we can't lose.
It's in the falling that we gently find our way,
And it is together that we will make a difference today.

So, let's begin our journey that is each snowflake's fate,
Heading toward Earth, we'll see the difference we make.
The effect we have will be felt by many,
And for me, dear friends, that will be plenty.

# Snowflake
## Being In the Moment (Mindfulness)

Snowflake's dilemma is deciding where she should land on earth to have the most impact so people will notice her when she falls. Her plan includes researching all the books at the library. When she does not come up with any answers, she decides to ask the Snow Princess to see if she has any ideas on where Snowflake should land. The Snow Princess tells Snowflake to stop putting emphasis on the final goal and just enjoy the experience of being in the moment.

# Snowflake
## Story Guide

1. Suggested words and phrases for discussion (Define):
   Acting versus reacting
   Being prepared versus lack of planning
   Compulsive versus impulsive
   Rigidity versus flexibility
   Thoughtful action versus thoughtless action

2. How do some of these phrases apply or don't apply to Snowflake? Discuss these words with your family or friends.
   "Jumping the gun"
   "Make the most of each moment"
   "Short term goals versus long term goals"
   "Take the time to smell the roses"
   "You can't see the forest for the trees".

3. Can too much planning and thinking take the fun out of something you are going to do? Who in your family or group of friends plans too much? Who doesn't plan enough? What about you?

4. Is it more important for Snowflake to find an important landing place or for Snowflake to enjoy the fall to earth? Which would be more important to you? Why?

5. Pretend you are Snowflake falling to Earth. Describe using your sense of touching, hearing, seeing, smelling and tasting the experience of the voyage. Describe each sensation as you close your eyes and feel like you are falling through the sky. Have your family or friends do the same.

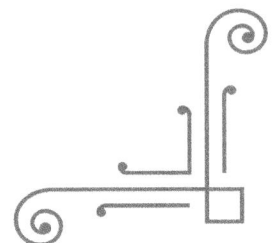

# Reflections

6. What do you think Snowflake's family and friends thought about her change in attitude? Have you ever changed your mind about something? Share the experience with your family or friends. Is it okay to change your mind sometimes? When is not okay?

7. What was the advice that the Snow Princess gave to Snowflake? Was it good advice? What would you have told Snowflake to do?

8. Draw a picture of what earth might look like from Heavenly Gate? Draw a picture of Heavenly Gate. Draw a picture of the Snow Princess.

9. Have a family member or friend put on some soft music. Begin to dance like a Snowflake. Close your eyes and feel like you are falling to the earth. Afterwards, each of you describe the feelings you experienced using the words think, see and feel with each description.

# KLINKER THE RAINBOW CLOWN

## (Theme: Diversity)

**CHORUS**

It is hard being different. Klinker often wondered why he was born that way. Other clowns had beautiful, one-colored faces. Charlie had a sparkling green face as bright as an emerald ring and so environmentally friendly. Felicia's face was a shocking pink and she had long, dark lashes to set off her delicate face. Billy was wonderful as Baby Blue. All the people loved him so much. Blue is so peaceful, Klinker thought. Buster Bobby had a bright red costume to match his bold-looking face of Red; a color with courage. Each color has a special meaning, so each clown knew his or her purpose. But not Klinker. The audience would applaud and squeals of delight rang from the children as the clowns entered the main ring on circus night. For Klinker no one squealed or laughed; they would simply sit in silence. Klinker felt like a failure. One night, Klinker decided he could not face another audience, so with a knapsack over his shoulder Klinker slipped out the back of the circus tent and headed down the road, alone and on his own. As day began to turn into night, Klinker became a little scared and he thought about the clowns who were probably eating a nice, hot dinner and talking about their grand day in the circus ring. Klinker shrugs and signs. In the deep forest Klinker sits down under a large tree.

**KLINKER**

Oh well, I would not have been included anyway.
I am better off alone; I think I am glad I didn't stay.

**OSCAR the OWL**

Little boy, you aren't alone,
Can't you see this is my home?

**KLINKER**

Who said that - should I be afraid of you?
Don't hurt me - I already feel blue.

**OSCAR the OWL**

It's just little me.
Up here in this tall tree.

**KLINKER**

What are you doing up so late at night?
You gave me quite a fright!

**OSCAR the OWL**

I could ask you the same thing.
Little boy with a striped face.
What are you doing in this quiet place?

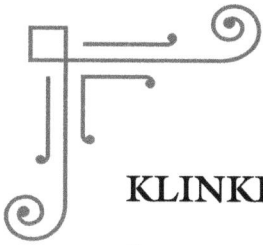

## KLINKER

I am running away from my circus home.
I've been traveling all day and I'm all alone.
My face is striped; not a color of one.
I've quit the circus. I'm through. I'm done.
I'm going where my face won't be strange
And my heart wont' feel so much pain.

## OSCAR the OWL

Hmmm, let me come closer for a better look.

## CHORUS

Oscar the Owl said as the tree branch shook.
With a flutter and a sigh,
Oscar landed on the ground nearby.

## OSCAR the OWL

It doesn't seem such a problem to me.
All those colors are a pleasure to see.

## KLINKER

No one understands and I just want to cry,
I feel so alone so I just said good-bye.
To everyone at the circus, they were called friend,
but the pain of being different had to end.

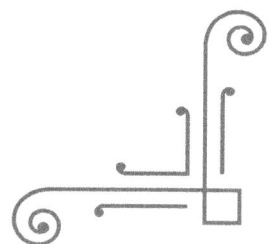

## OSCAR the OWL

Now don't do that; in the morning you'll see a bright new sky.
And your life may seem different from this mountain high.
The forest friends will help mend your heart.
So, go to sleep and tomorrow we will start.

## KLINKER

Thank you, Oscar. Yes, I will lie down and try to sleep.
It is my prayer the pain will disappear; this pain so deep.

## CHORUS

Klinker beds down beneath the tree,
While Oscar sits on his favorite branch his eyes opened to see,
He will stand watch and comfort the clown.
This little boy who seems so sad, so down.
The morning comes and Klinker opens one eye.
Today may be different; maybe Klinker won't cry.

## KLINKER

I guess the owl must have left during the night.
Maybe he left out of fright.
Well I better be on my way.
I can't stay here all day.

**CHORUS**

Suddenly Oscar swoops down and lands next to Klinker and reassures him.

**OSCAR the OWL**

My friends are coming to figure out a plan,
They're all willing to extend a helping hand.

**KLINKER**

Oh, I thought you had flown away,
And there didn't seem any reason for me to stay.
I was just ready to hit the road.
With this burden on me, it feels like a heavy load.

**CHORUS**

Klinker finds himself surrounded by curious forest animals.

**OSCAR the OWL**

Come gather around each and every friend.
We need to tell Klinker what we recommend.
Klinker is looking for a new home.
Should he stop here or continue to roam?
Wee Willie Raccoon, what do you think he should do?
Do you think Klinker has a problem or two?

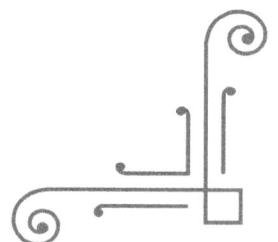

## CHORUS

Wee Willie the Raccoon shakes head with a quizzical look,
as he settled himself in a moss-covered nook.

## KLINKER

You don't understand.
The circus children are not my fans.
They don't laugh and they never smile,
I do my best all the while.
Every clown has a special color.
And they know how important they are,
Each clown in the circus is a star.
I just have silly stripes all over my face.
I feel so out of place.
I want to be a famous clown,
To make people happy in every town.
I don't know why I am this way.
Do any of you have something to say?

## CHORUS

The dainty little flowers sitting in the field couldn't understand,
Why did Klinker think he didn't have a fan?

## FLOWERS in the FIELD

We have colors - colors galore.
We wouldn't mind if we had more.
So Klinker, why do you care?
See all the colors that we share.

## CHORUS

Klinker sunk in to the deep bed of flowers and began to cry.
Klinker just can't figure out why.
Everyone should be laughing at the circus; having fun.
No one laughs at him and he is just done.

## KLINKER

But I'm not a flower.
There are many colors for you to share.
I know your kind words are because you care.
But all your colors are on my face.
I'm so embarrassed. I feel disgraced.

## GENTLE MOTHER DOE

Look at me, my coat is colors of many.
All these browns, so full and plenty.
I am proud of my colors, and I have quite a few;
There are brown, some white and some black ones too.

## KLINKER

Oh, you are beautiful, my sweet doe.
If I looked like you, I wouldn't feel so low.
Your colors blend ever so nice.
You don't look like me with every color spliced.

## CHORUS

As the forest friends are trying to understand
Klinker's problem, and create a plan, dark clouds begin to form.

## OSCAR the OWL

Hold everything, Gang!
Here comes the storm. Here comes the rain!
Run for cover! Run for cover!
Head for the cave. That's where we will hover.

## CHORUS

Klinker ran with the animals in to a small, warm cave.
This is where they will stay until the weather begins to behave.
The water begins to pour and the trees are whipped by the wind.
Everyone huddles, feeling frightened from friend to friend.
Their bodies shake as they cover their ears from the lightening strike,
No one knows for sure if they ever will be rid of this fright.
The old weather man is angry indeed.
No let up, no one will be free.
Until this storm passes away from here,
Everyone keeps holding hands; feeling their fear.
Shaking and shattering, tree branches ripping from the trunk.
No one knows what is in store - will they all be sunk?
Whipping in a frenzy, water everywhere,

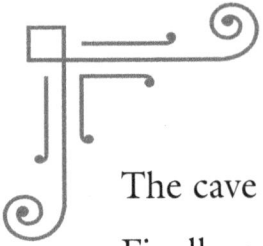

The cave is the only safe haven, the forest friends will be spared.

Finally, a new day brought out the sun,
and the animals come out one by one.
As the leaves on the trees begin to dry,
Klinker begins to wonder why.

**KLINKER**

Look at the strange colors in the sky?
Look dear forest friends — turn your eyes up high.
These colors seem to comfort me.
I don't know why but I am feeling free.

**CHORUS**

The Rainbow Voice speaks.

**RAINBOW VOICE**

This rainbow is my promise a bridge will be there.
to show when you need me, that I really care.
The rainbow bridge comes from deep in my heart.
To show my love for you that will never depart.
Remember Klinker, my rainbow's gift shines on your face.
Like the joy of creation that will never be erased.
And you Klinker, as your face reflects this gift,
Be a bridge, bring happiness to those who need a lift.
You can feel what each person feels,
You can help solve their problems; then they can heal.
Go home now and do your part,
And a smile within, you can start.
You'll be surprised how many hearts you will mend.
Don't you know you are the perfect blend?

## CHORUS

Klinker stands and stares at the rainbow for a time.
Hmmm — is this message helping him feel fine?
He is beginning to realize the importance of his colored face.
He is a bridge helping everyone to come together in one place.

The forest friends know Klinker has been given a gift,
Just watching his smiling face gives them a lift.

## FOREST FRIENDS

Klinker, you have courage and your face radiates love.
You will create magic, just like the rainbow above.

## CHORUS

With those words of encouragement from the forest friends.
Klinker knows his quest in finding himself has come to an end.
He knows who he is and he feels proud in the knowing,
His multi-striped face is actually glowing.
He waves good-bye and heads for the road.
His knapsack over his shoulder doesn't feel like a load.
He picks up his feet and begins a steady pace.
He is anxious to return to the circus and show his rainbow face.

## CHORUS

Under the circus tent, the clowns are arguing with one another,
and Baby Blue lets' out a shout,

## BABY BLUE CLOWN

Look guys, it is the return of our brother.
Klinker is here and we have nothing left to fear.
Now everything will be alright.
Okay fellows, stop this fight.

## CHORUS

The clowns surround Klinker, all talking together.
It has been a difficult time to weather.
The people didn't come.
Klinker had been the center of the fun.

## KLINKER

Well, that seems strange and I don't know what is going on,
I ran away from the circus because I didn't think I belonged.
No one laughed when they saw me.
What is different from the way it used to be?

## BUSTER BOBBY

You never told us why you didn't smile.
We figured that was your special style.
But people love you the way you are.
Among us, you're the brightest and best star.
People missed you and wouldn't come back.
Without you, they felt a curious lack.
Of something special that only you gave.
Klinker, your talent is in the way you behave.
You never criticize and always seem so wise.
You have a way of knowing our feelings.
And you do it without ever revealing,
Our deepest secrets and fears.
We've grown so fond of you over the years.
You have been an inspiration and model to all,
It makes everyone want to respond to the highest call.
We have learned you are the common link.
To each of us it's important what you feel and think.
Your face shows a reflection we are not alone,
and together we're a family Klinker, so welcome home!

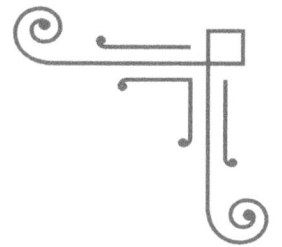

# Klinker,
# The Rainbow Clown

## Diversity

Klinker the Clown has a multi-striped face. All the other clowns have solid color faces. Klinker feels very different and decides to run away from the circus. During his time away from the circus he talks to the forest animals about his being different. He is not able to convince them about the seriousness of his problem. When the Rainbow Voice talks to Klinker, he realizes he does not have a problem and he begins to understand how he brings people together and he appreciates his ability to do this in life.

# Klinker,
# The Rainbow Clown
## Story Guide

1.  Why do you think the forest animals didn't think Klinker had a problem? Do you think Klinker had a problem? What would you have told him?

2.  Why do you think Klinker felt so different? Would you feel different if you were Klinker? Do you ever feel different? What are you thinking when you feel different? Share this with your family or friends.

3.  Have your family or friends pick out a special face color paint. Make up your face in a color or colors. Have everyone dress up in clown costumes and visit a hospital and entertain children or elderly people.

4.  What is your favorite color? What does blue mean to you? Red? Yellow? Green? Pink? Brown? Black?

## Reflections

5.  Take different colors of construction paper and make a rainbow. Paste the different colors on a large sheet of paper and hang it in your room. At the end of the rainbow write a special wish that you want to come true. Every time you look at your rainbow with the wish, say the wish out loud with your eyes closed. Try to say the wish at least once each day.

6.  Put on music so you can close your eyes and picture what type of colors go with the music being played. Pretend you are looking at a kaleidoscope, and seeing the different colored configurations. Have your family or friends join in this exercise with you. After you are through, draw the pictures you saw and then talk about the experience with each other.

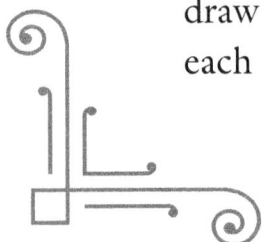

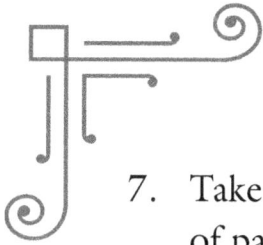

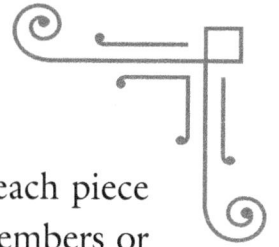

7. Take small pieces of paper and write a different color on each piece of paper. Put the papers in a bowl and have your family members or friends select a paper. Have everyone act out what they think the color means. Example: red might mean anger or being bold while blue might be peaceful or cool. See if the other members of your group can guess the color you are trying to play.

8. Plan to wear a blouse or shirt that matches your mood for a certain day. Example: Wear a pink blouse if you are "feeling in the pink" that particular day or wear a red shirt if you are trying to have extra courage that day.

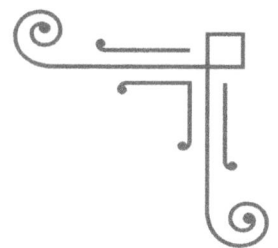

# SHY VIOLET

## (Theme: Self-Esteem)

**CHORUS**

In the winter the beautiful flowers hid in their leaves so the chilly air would not harm their soft petals. The flowers always looked forward to the first day of Spring so they could begin to blossom, filling the fields with a rainbow of color. Even now, through their leaves, they sometimes peek out to see what new plants had arrived in their community. Engaging Iris who is peeking out from her leaves, says:

**IRIS**

I wonder who the new flower over there might be?
Do you think she'll pop out so we can see?
There is no way to tell if she is pretty or plain.
Her leaves are different; they seem quite strange.

**CHORUS**

Tilly the Tulip chimes in.

**TILLY the TULIP**

You're right, Iris. I was watching her too.
I wonder if she's going to be big and bright?
Or just a plain Jane.
That won't last the night?

**CHORUS**

Sweet Susie the Carnation intervenes.

**SWEET SUSIE THE CARNATION**

Now girls, be careful what you say.
Let's not pre-judge.
Let's wait for the big day!

**IRIS**

It doesn't make any difference, I guess.
This time tomorrow we'll join the rest.
Of the flowers and become a blooming hill.
People will come to see us, they get such a thrill.

**CHORUS**

Next day, it is an early morning sunrise. The field began to glow with a rainbow of colors. All were blooming except the little new arrival with the velvet green leaves still hiding her face in this special place.

Marigold shouts…

**MARIGOLD**

Hey, you in those leaves.
Come out and be seen.
You have nothing to worry about and nothing to fear.
Come on out, do you hear?

**CHORUS**

The little plant continues to hide.
What is going on with this one inside?
No one can figure out about this little flower.
She sure looks afraid and continues to cower.

The Snapdragon snaps:

**SNAPDRAGON**

Strange, strange little plant.
Maybe it's impossible to bloom and she just can't.

**CHORUS**

The little Periwinkle says with a puzzled ton

**PERIWINKLE**

Don't be silly, all flowers bloom.
She'll probably come out and very soon.

**DAISY**

Let's act calmly.
Perhaps our new neighbor is not very tough.
I'll begin with an introduction or two.
Perhaps if I talk gently,
She'll come out on our cue.
Hello, my name is Daisy. Welcome to our home.
We gladly accept you as one of our own.
We saw your seed land on the ground.
If you'll come out - you'll see flowers all around.

## CHORUS

Very quietly the leaves began to part.
and a little Violet poked her head out from the dark.

## SHY VIOLET

Can I really blend in here?
Something tells me I am feeling a lot of fear.
This is all new and very strange indeed.
Can you tell me, are there more violet seeds?
Am I alone or did my family come too?
The last thing I remember was a great wind that blew.

## DAISY

You are the only violet here.
But don't worry you can live in our field.
We are the flowers of Flower Hill.
We plant our seeds among the grass.
So that our children will grow and last.
With our color, fragrance and soft touch.
People come from all around,
Just to see our beauty covering the ground.
Seeds flying through the air.
Flower seeds are everywhere.
And they always find places to land.
From the mountain top to the dessert sand.

**SHY VIOLET**

Thank you for welcoming me to this beautiful place.
Can I stay here in this warm space?

**DAISY**

Just enjoy our patch of sunny field.
If you are hurt or sad, the warm sun will help you heal.

**CHORUS**

The darling little Daffodil cheerfully says:

**DARLING LITTLE DAFFODIL**

We are one big happy family.
We have no fights and we never make a fuss,
You are welcome to stay with us.

**SHY VIOLET**

You seem to enjoy each other.
I would be proud to join too.
However, I may not have much to offer you.

## CHORUS

Tiger Lily roars at Shy Violet...

## TIGER LILY

Well, that doesn't sound right.
Don't put yourself down.
You are a beautiful purple but you do seem shy.
Would you be willing to tell us why?

## SHY VIOLET

I just don't know how to talk and I often feel left out.
Around beautiful flowers I have nothing to tout.
I'm so little and I'm most often overlooked.

## CHORUS

Shy Violet lowers her head as she shook.

## ORCHID

You seem to doubt yourself.
Why not begin to be like me.
I am the famous Orchid.
Pinned to evening gowns for all the world to see.

**RED ROSE**

Well I can top that, I am the famous red rose.
When I arrive, everyone glows.
Women in their prime.
Wish for me all the time.

**DAISY**

Let little Violet talk.
What happened to you?
Did someone say something.
To make you feel blue?

**SHY VIOLET**

I doubt myself and I am very shy.
There must be some reason.
but I don't know why.
And I don't know that even if I knew.
My shyness would end, so I could be like you.

**CHORUS**

The Bachelor Buttons say with concern in their voice:

## BACHELOR BUTTONS

Well, we can't have our flowers feeling bad.
We appreciate your shy little self so don't be sad.
Don't apologize for who you are.
Please, little Violet - you could be a star

## CHORUS

The pretty Poinsettias tell Shy Violet:

## PRETTY POINSETTIAS

Maybe you were meant for a flower shop.
Perhaps by your store window, people would stop.
But then if you never believed in you,
It's not our job to keep you from feeling blue.
Maybe our purpose in the end,
Is simply just to be your friend.

## CHORUS

The Blue Bonnets chime in perfect time:

## BLUE BONNETS

We watch when some of us are chosen.
Some are packed in boxes and some are frozen.
You could fill a glorious vase,
You're beginning to sprout a lovely face.
You could be in a bouquet of flowers,
Picked before the first Spring shower.

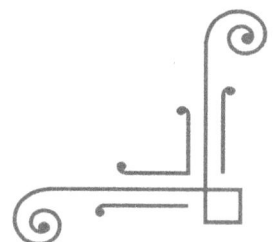

## SHY VIOLET

I don't care what I will be.
No matter what, customers won't pick me.

## CHORUS

And Motherly Mumm comforts Shy Violet:

## MOTHERLY MUMM

Please don't feel such despair.
Can't you see, we really do care.
Each flower has a different personality.
We accept you just as you are.
You don't need to be a star.
We'll believe in you as you grow,
Even if you have trouble accepting what we know.

## SHY VIOLET

You believe in me just as I am?
You act as if you are my fans.

## CHORUS

Gladys the Gladiola gives Shy Violet advice:

## GLADYS THE GLADIOLA

We must ask the Noble Wise One.
He'll tell us what happened to you.
We'll get to the bottom of this once and for all.
Just keep your stem straight and stand ever so tall.

## SHY VIOLET

What Wise One can we ask?
Who could handle this difficult task?

## GLADYS THE GLADIOLA

We will talk to the ancient Oak.
His roots grow very deep.
And we know he never sleeps.
The old Oak will hear our plea.
And an answer forthcoming will be.
Why, oh why is Violet so shy?
She is cute and soft.
A pleasant little flower.
Why does she always hide and cower?

## CHORUS

No one knew what the old Oak would say,
but everyone waited for answers that day.
Time seemed to stand still,
as the flowers waited on Flower Hill.

Suddenly the ground began to shake and rocks rumbled.
from the hillside in a great tumble.
The trees swayed, and the river splashed.
Animals became frightened and began to dash.
Then the Old Oak's voice bellowed through the air.
And everyone froze in their tracks.
No one moved; no one dared.

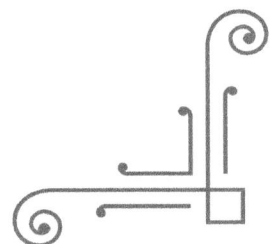

## WISE OLD OAK

What is this talk about not being worthwhile?
Everything on Earth should wear a smile.
All creatures were created by a plan.
Who is questioning what they don't understand

## CHORUS

Shy Violet stood very still.
The voice she had heard came from the top of the hill.
She had hoped her friends might intervene.
Protecting her from this frightful scene.
No one spoke, and everyone quivered inside.
Little Violet knew of no place to hide.
She finally opened her petals to speak.
Leaves shaking like chattering teeth.

## SHY VIOLET

I am the one who feels unworthy to live.
Here in flower field I have nothing to give.
I have been shy all my life and I doubt
that I am part of any special plan.
Do you understand?

## WISE OLD OAK

You make me sad, my little flower.
Because you feel you have no power.
No one can convince you of your worth.
You're very important on this earth.
No one can make you believe against your will.
You must decide how you feel.
Your value is what you want it to be.
Make a choice and you will see.

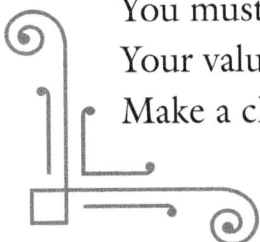

## SHY VIOLET

You mean it is up to me what I believe?
I can be happy and decide what I want to achieve?

## WISE OLD OAK

That's right for thoughts are strong.
If you're not careful you can choose wrong.
If you need to feel bad about who you are.
you can be a failure and not be a star.
It's up to you. You could be great.
The choice is yours alone to make.

## SHY VIOLET

Well, I've wasted much time.
Thinking sad thoughts.
And to myself not being kind
I want to reach my highest good.
What you are saying is now understood.
I am beginning to know I am worth a great deal.
And it is through your advice I will now heal.
I choose a life that is worth living,
Sharing with others and giving.
After all, no one else has my face.
I believe I deserve a special place.
So, I will open my petals.
and smile at the glorious sun,
knowing I have only just now begun.

# Shy Violet
## Self-Esteem

Shy Violet finds herself in a field of bright and beautiful flowers. She decides she is not as pretty as the others so she refuses to bloom. The flowers in the field decide to ask the wise Old Oak what Shy Violet should do about not feeling pretty. Through the Wise Oaks' advice, Shy Violet begins to understand how her thoughts have the ultimate control over how she sees herself and her life.

# Shy Violet
## Story Guide

1   Why do you think Shy Violet didn't think she was worthwhile? What did the other flowers say to her that made her feel better? Have you ever felt like Shy Violet? Share your answer with a trusted person and see if the two of you can find an answer to make you feel better.

2.  What advice did the flowers give Shy Violet? What advice would you have given to her?

3.  Who was the one who gave Shy Violet wise advice? Who gives you wise advice in life? Do you follow it? Think about advice you have been given and did you follow it? Did you think it was wise? If not, why?

4.  Make a list of ways in which you feel powerless and not good about yourself. Then make a list of ways in which you feel powerful. Then close your eyes and see yourself in powerful situations that make you feel good.

## Reflections

5.  Have your family or friends close their eyes along with you doing the same. Think about a fear you have. Try to draw a picture in your mind about what that fear looks like. What does it sound like? How do you think it became your worse fear? With your eyes still closed, see yourself walking up to the fear and smiling at the fear. Think about turning the fear in to a friend. How would you do that? What would the picture look like now? How would it sound? How would you know that it is now your friend? Have a trusted person guide you through this journey so your eyes can be closed while the questions are being asked.

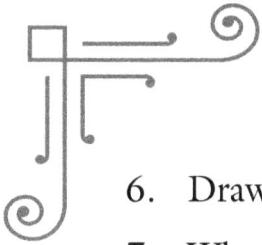

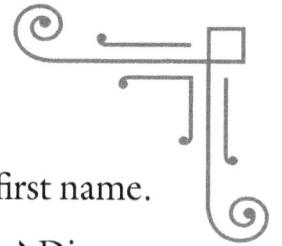

6. Draw a field of flowers and give each of the flowers a special first name.

7. What type of flower would you be if you could be any flower? Discuss this with your family or friends. Have everyone pick a flower they would like to be and have them explain why they picked that flower.

8. Take turns with your family or friends standing in front of a mirror and saying positive statements that describe who you are. Example: I am a smart person. I have a good sense of humor. People like me.

9. Go to a field of flowers and pick a bouquet to give to someone very special in your life. If you don't live near a field, buy a bouquet at a flower shop and share the flowers with that special person.

10. Wear a fresh flower in your hair or in your lapel every day for a week. Carry some fresh flowers with you and share them with people you meet for the first time that day.

# THE MUSICAL MIRACLE MERRY-GO-ROUND

## (Theme: Achieve Ability to Believe)

### CHORUS

All the Children knew it was a special merry-go-round. So, they spent every Saturday riding it. None of the parents understood why the children loved the merry-go-round so much but the children knew it was very special. Many, many miracles surrounded the multi-colored machine in the center of the park. The children always asked David to go with them but David wouldn't waste his time with such foolishness. After all, he was ten-years-old and his mother had told him that he was the man of the house now that his father had left home to find a new job. The paper mill had shut down a few weeks before and the company had laid off David's father. David had chores and couldn't waste time riding on those phony ponies. After school, he would race home to unlock the door for his sister Katie. Then David would race to the local store where he would deliver groceries around town. After dinner, he and Katie would do their homework. David was a serious student. At night David would be up late studying and his mother would come in to his room and insist he turn off his light and get some sleep. Every night David would dream about his father who he missed very much. They had not heard from him for a while and David knew his mother was very worried. He thought about searching for his father but he would not leave his mother and Katie. With the covers up around his ears to keep the chill away, David slipped in to a deep sleep. The next morning a beautiful sparrow was sitting on David's windowsill.

**SPARROW**

Come follow me... Come follow me.
To wonderful, exciting new worlds. Just wait and see.

**CHORUS**

David hurriedly slips in to his clothes and raced down the hall to Katie's room.

**DAVID**

Wake up! Something strange has happened to me,
Hurry up, come and see.

**KATIE**

What are you saying David my dear,
You said a bird was talking; what did you hear?

**DAVID**

Yes, a sparrow talked to me in my room.
Honest, he talked or at least I assume.

**KATIE**

I am coming so let me get dressed.
What is going on, I can't even guess.

## CHORUS

As David and Katie run down the hall.
They heard the sparrow give one last call.
They run into David's room,
The sparrow was beginning to croon.

## SPARROW

Anyone wanting to travel along,
Better heed this special song.
Oh, you've brought your sister to join in the fun.
Well, don't take too long — here comes the Sun!

## DAVID

How can this be,
A bird talking to you and me?
I must be dreaming.
I better crawl back in to bed,
and pull the covers up over my head.

## KATIE

Didn't you listen to the little bird?
You act like he wasn't even heard.
Hurry, there isn't very much time.
Everyone is waiting by the entrance sign.

## DAVID

Go away, Katie, this is just a dream.
It can't be more than what it seems.

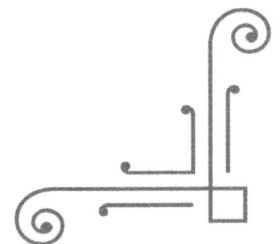

## KATIE

Well, if its' just a dream, why not come along
And join in the Sparrow's song?

## CHORUS

David thinks for a moment in time.
It couldn't hurt and it might be just fine.
David jumps out of his bed.
He changes his mind instead.
As David and Katie approach the park gate,
It looks like they may have to wait.
On the Musical Merry-Go-Round they want to ride.
The sparrow is pointing to it with a loud cry.
A gold ring dangles very high.
And the children grab the air as they pass by.
Grabbing the gold ring was the neatest of all,
the children stretch and stand ever so tall.
Now it is Katie and David's turn.
What will they each learn?
Katie squeals with delight,
But David appears to be feeling some fright.

## DAVID

Why try to grab the gold ring?
It's a lot of work for such a small thing.

**KATIE**

Come on David, it's a surprise you can't even guess.
It's greater and bigger and always the best!

**CHORUS**

Katie jumps on a pretty little pinto and gallops away.
No time to sit around; no time to just stay.
David chooses a stallion, a rare horse with pride.
He has chosen wisely; this horse he will ride.
The horse's mane soft as a feather.
The saddle was made of genuine leather.
The stirrups shone brightly.
Their silver caps covered his toes very tightly.

**DAVID**

My goodness, this horse is real, I think.
I believe I just saw him blink.

**CHORUS**

As the horse tossed its' head and mane with a fling.
He snickered at David and said,

## DAVID'S HORSE

Don't you believe in anything?
Of course, I am real — start to believe.
And you may see what is real.
It is time to go - it is time to feel.

## DAVID

I don't know whether I will last.
But this merry-go-round is going too fast.
So, I guess I'm here for this time.
I don't know what I will find.
I wonder should I reach for the gold ring.
It seems like a silly thing.

## CHORUS

As David's horse tells David to go ahead and find a way,
then they won't have to travel in circles all day.

## DAVID

How can you know what I am thinking?
And look your eyes are still blinking.

## DAVID'S HORSE

You are a strange boy, doubting David.
Usually the first question children ask me,
Is how can I talk? How can that be?

## DAVID

Well, I have never heard of a horse that could talk.
The only ones I know can just gallop or walk.
This is such a strange dream.
I might as well reach for the gold ring.

## DAVID'S HORSE

That a boy, go for the ring; You'll see,
There is a new world waiting for you and me.

## CHORUS

The Merry-go-round whirled and twirled.
The music played so loud,
The children's line became quite the crowd.
The circles of color began to blend and music filled the air.
Laughter from the children showed how much they cared.

## DAVID'S HORSE

Okay, David, here's your chance.
The ring is near, reach out— oh dear.
That won't do; I need the ring to fly with you.
If you don't hurry, David, the music will end.
And your ride will be over,
And we'll have to part, dear friend.

**CHORUS**

Around the circle they went again,
Children's hair flying in the wind.
David missed again; he didn't know it would be so hard.
The gold ring was high and to reach was so far.

**DAVID**

I'm trying, but it seems so far away.
I'm afraid I'll have to try another day.

**CHORUS**

As they came around once more,
David struggled to clasp the ring.
He felt his fingers wrap around.
As he almost fell to the ground.

**DAVID'S HORSE**

Hold on tight, David and off we'll go.
Now you're in for a spectacular show.

**CHORUS**

David held the reins ever so tight.
Then glanced down and saw the ring on his hand, the right.

**DAVID**

I got it! I got it!

## CHORUS

David yelled to his friends,
and then with his horse, they leaped toward earth's end.
A rainbow appeared, as David flew through the sky.

## DAVID

Oh, how beautiful!
I didn't know what it felt like to fly.

## CHORUS

The horse spread his wings as his hoofs left the ground.
And behind them was a child's laughter as the only sound.
Higher and higher they flew on their way.
David was speechless; he had nothing further to say,
They continued to climb up through the clouds.
For David it was a magical day,
But as he looked down below, he began to sway.
He began to tumble over and over.
into a field of poppies and clover.

The poppies felt like a cushion, all soft and serene.
"Ah" David exclaimed, feeling like a king.
He saw children running, laughing and playing.
Come on David, they were all saying.
You haven't seen anything yet.
We have a lot to do before the sun sets.
David and the children ran through the fields.
With them by their side they reached the top of the hill.
Ice cream of many flavors flowed down one side.
David was delighted as the children raced by.

Gooey chocolate ran down like a river.
with pineapple and strawberry in between.
It was the most amazing thing he had ever seen.

**CHILDREN**

Dig in, dig in, eat all you can,
It comes straight from the ice cream man.

**CHORUS**

The children slid down the hill.
The magic ride was a wonderful thrill.
As David and his friends left behind the ice cream land.
They headed toward a forest that looked quite grand.
They ran through the woods made of gumdrop trees.
With honeysuckle blossoms buzzing with bees.
The bark was made with licorice and sugar cones.
With so many sweets they didn't think about going home.
Every flower in the world danced around their feet.
This was the moment when they would finally meet.
The Queen of the Ice Light Castle Store.
Who would grant each child one wish, but no more.

One by one the children went forward.
One child chose a new house for his family of five.
And another chose joy for as long as he was alive.
David came last. The Queen smiled at him.
David knew his wish must be serious; not a whim.

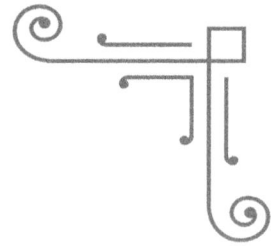

**QUEEN of Ice Light Castle Store**

What do you wish for David? What do you hold true?
What is it that I can give only to you?

**DAVID**

I wish for one thing alone.
Can you bring my father home?

**QUEEN of Ice Light Castle Store**

Well David, such a request is worth the try.

**CHORUS**

And with that, David's dream flew by in the blink of an eye.

David was back in his bed with spinning in his groggy head.

**DAVID**

Oh, my mother is calling my name.
Where have I been - was it just a game?
I better get up and get dressed.
Oh, that is strange - I have my clothes on,
And I am home where I belong.
But more than half the day is gone.
Ice cream hills, gumdrops and gee,
Honey suckle and buzzing bees.
Such a dream - such a dream.
Much more than what it seems.

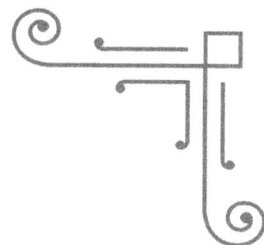

## CHORUS

David gets up and makes his bed.
All the while scratching his head.
So strange, a sparrow singing a song.
Calling me to come along.
Riding a horse and grabbing the gold ring.
All of this seems more than just a dream.
David joins Katie and mom as they share time,
In the kitchen sitting together and suddenly he finds,
The sparrow sitting on the windowsill.
Singing the sweetest melody, the room with music is filled.
Suddenly the door opens and in walks David's dad.
Everyone is talking and smiling, no one is sad.

## DAVID'S DAD

I received a call from a lady today.
What happened next is hard to say.
The lady had a strange dream.
She said it was much more than what it seemed.
This lady owns the local house of ice.
She needs someone to manage the store and be nice.
The lady said something strange indeed.
She said that in her dream,
There was a visit from a Queen.
She said she was to hire me and she said something more.
The Queen said the man to hire has a son by the name of David,
Who has finally achieved the ability to believe.

# The Musical Miracle Merry-Go-Round

## Achieve Ability to Believe

David's father travels to another city looking for work. He is gone for a long time, and David is upset by his father's absence. One day David is invited to ride on the Musical Miracle Merry-Go-Round. Although David has heard that the Musical Miracle Merry-Go-Round is magical, he doesn't believe it even after he grabs the gold ring and strange things begin to happen to him. Through the efforts of the Ice Light Castle Store Queen, David 's father comes home and David finally achieves the ability to believe in Miracles.

# The Musical Miracle
# Merry-Go-Round
## Story Guide

1. David's father had been gone for a long time looking for work in another town. Was David sad because his father was gone? Was Katie upset about her father being gone? How might they have shown they were feeling sad?

2. Did David and Katie talk to their mother about their father being gone? What could they and their mother have said or done to each other to make themselves feel better during their father's absence?

3. David was a very responsible ten-year-old boy. Did David have fun with so much responsibility? Was David resentful for having to be so responsible? Are you responsible for chores in your home? What are they?

4. The gold ring was the highlight of the Musical Miracle Merry-Go-Round? Why was the gold ring such a prize? At first David did not seem very interested in the gold ring. What might have made David feel that way? What type of attitude did David have about getting the gold ring? How did his attitude hinder or help David in getting the ring?

5. The Ice Light Castle Store Queen granted a wish to each child. The story mentioned some of the wishes. What might have been some wishes not mentioned in the story? Name the most unusual wish a child in the story could have asked for?

6. David thought his dream was make believe rather than real until something special happened. What was the special event that made David believe?

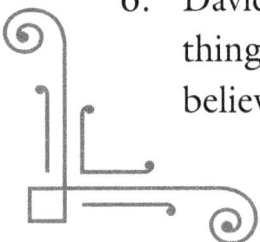

# Reflections

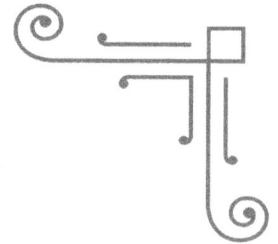

7. Take yourself or go with a group of friends to a Merry-go-Round. Close your eyes as you ride faster and let your imagination take you on a journey to your own special land.

8. Keep a dream journal next to your bed so you can record your dreams. Share a recent dream with a group of friends or family members. Try to interpret the dream by replacing the main characters or objects in the dream with yourself.

9. How can the dream be interpreted from those different viewpoints? Have the group help you understand the dream. If the dream was a bad or incomplete dream, before going to sleep, use your imagination so the dream can have a positive outcome and be completed.

10. Goal setting gives us focus and a plan of action. Think of something in your life that you want very much. Make a list of three goals with at least five small and five large steps that it would take to achieve those goals. Work on each step until that step is completed. Then move to the next step. Example: a college degree might mean sending for a school brochure and selecting one or more classes. Another step might be in making an appointment with a school counselor to talk about your goals and the steps needed to reach the goals.

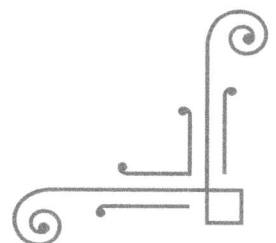

# BUTTERCUP AND THE BEAUTY CONTEST

## (Theme: Competition)

### CHORUS

The Ferndale forest air was filled with excitement. Spring was just around the corner and the forest friends were a twitter with preparation for the contest coming soon. The butterfly beauty contest was always a popular event. Oh, there were plenty of other contests in the forest but none as breathtakingly beautiful as the butterfly contest. The great elk competed each year, clanging and banging their horns to see who was the strongest one of all. The chipmunks competed to see who could chatter the longest and loudest in the chipmunk chatter contest. Even the beavers had a building contest to see which beaver was the best worker in the forest. Every year competition became stiffer and this year appeared to not be any different.

The butterflies wrapped away in the cocoon.
Will they be coming out; will it be soon?
How much longer will the forest friends have to wait?
Which butterfly will win and fulfill his fate?
Bird songs are filling the Spring and gentle air.
How will the annual contest be managed; will it be fair?
What is going on - will be it be soon?
Will the butterflies be coming out before the full moon?

### BUTTERCUP the BUTTERFLY

(Whispers to Oscar the Owl sitting in the tree)
There is something that is dreadfully wrong.
We want to come out, but first there is something,
about which we feel so strong.

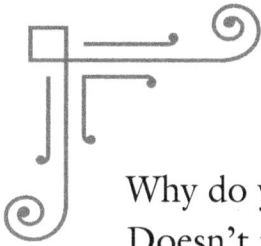

Why do you have beauty contests each year?
Doesn't that just create separation and fear?
We have been talking for days on end.
And we don't want to compete since we are friends.
Please find out if compete we must.
We may not want to put up with all this fuss.

**CHORUS**

Oscar the Owl gives out a shout.

**OSCAR the OWL**

Oh goodness sakes, my dear.
We've held contests each and every year!
We love to look at each of you.
Your colors are so vivid, bright and true.
Please don't let me hear you say,
that you will continue to hide away.

**BUTTERCUP the BUTI'ERFLY**

We think this contest may be a sin!
We all lose when only one can win.
Talk to your friends and let us know.
We would rather not participate in your show.

**OSCAR the OWL**

I will do my best.
But this will be a very tough test.
I'll be back after I meet with the forest friends.
I'm not sure this is a rule we can bend.
By putting our heads together an answer we may gain.
But without a contest this forest won't be the same.

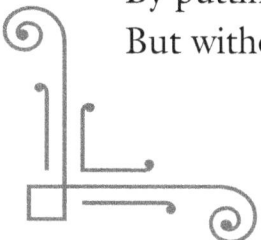

## CHORUS

Lulu, the Lavender Butterfly has a thing to say,
And Gabby the Green Butterfly shares thoughts in her own way.

## LULU, the LAVENDER BUTTERFLY

Oh, Buttercup I hope you are right.
Why do you think contests make everyone fight?
I would be willing to have everyone vote.
Perhaps I could win with my shiny purple coat.

## GABBY the GREEN BUTTERFLY

You might win, but so might I.
My green coat sparkles whenever I fly.

I come from a long line of beauties.
My mother was the winner just last year.
So, I have nothing to fear.

## CHORUS

Rippley the Reddish Butterfly lets' out a cry.

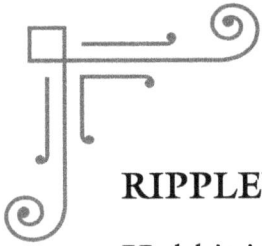

## RIPPLEY the REDDISH BUTTERLY

Hold it just a minute, Gabby and Lulu.
Buttercup and the others may be right,
And I'm willing to wait rather than fight.
After these contests many butterflies cry.
Because they think they don't even have a chance to try.
Others think that the judges were bought,
And some believe they're just in a tough spot.
Soon accusations start flying like crazy,
And friends hate friends.
Then everything becomes pretty hazy.

## BUTTERCUP the BUTTERFLY

We all agreed to strike to end this mess.
We are all winners and we should not allow such a test.
Let us be patient, until Oscar returns with the word.
By now the forest friends have probably heard.
We won't budge; we won't move an inch.
We'll stay where we are, that's a cinch.

## CHORUS

Meanwhile back in the forest deep.
Oscar and his friends go without sleep.
The Blue Mocking bird is heard:

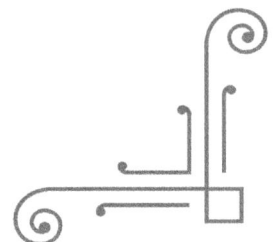

## BLUE MOCKING BIRD

What they are doing is totally absurd.
What do you mean the butterflies refuse to come out?
I am going to fly over to them and shout.

## CHORUS

Stanley the Skunk exclaims:

## STANLEY SKUNK

Mother Nature won't stand for this news.
She'll blow her stack; she will blow a fuse.

## OSCAR the OWL

I suppose we better visit Mother Nature now.
And tell her ourselves but I am not sure how.
Freddie the Fox and Delphia the Doe, will you volunteer with me?
Hey! Don't hide behind that tree.

## FREDDIE the FOX

Alright, alright I am willing to go!
But let me tell you it isn't going to be a pleasant show.
I'm a good talker, and perhaps with just a few more.
Can we fill Mother Nature in on the score?
That its' the butterflies' who need to be sct straight,
How many of us will join and together this path take?

## DELPHIA the DOE

I am a doe and I will go.
Along with me, that makes three.
One more will make it four.
And then we won't need anymore.

## CHORUS

Oscar, Freddie, Delphia and Bucky Beaver agree to go.

## BUCKY BEAVER

Sure, I'm not busy for the next few days.
The dam is built so I was just going to play.

## CHORUS

The forest friends decide to leave early the next day.
And throughout the night most of them decided to pray.
Oscar for sure stayed awake most of the night.
Among the animals the tension was tight.
As the sun peaked over the mountain top,
And the four began to march, resolving not to stop.
Hours passed and still they continued to walk.
Everyone seemed nervous and no one wanted to talk.
As the afternoon sun began to set,
The sky turned purple and the group continued the trek.

At last they reach a cliff with water rippling down the hill.
Oscar led the way, walking with care behind the spill.
This majestic waterfall, so perfect; so pristine.
Beautiful blue water, so cool and so clean.
Behind the fall, a dark cave appeared in their sight.
All of the forest friends were filled with fright.

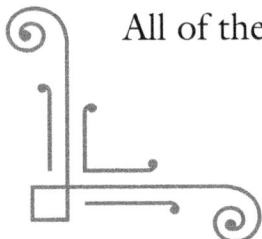

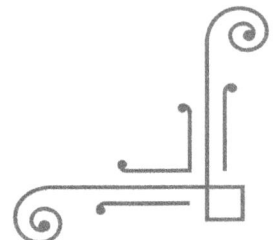

## CHORUS

Cave Guard and the forest friends meet.
They tell the Cave Guard it is Mother Nature they seek.

## CAVE GUARD

Where are you from?
And why to this place do you come?

## OSCAR the OWL

A major problem has brought us here.
Our butterflies refuse to compete.
So, we've come to Mother Nature to entreat.
She must make them stop their strike.
Or we'll never have another competitive fight.

## CHORUS

The guard told the group to be patient and wait.
They could stand by the entrance to the cave gate.
    With that a silence overtook the cave.
And the group of four weren't sure how to behave.
A short time later the guard said as he reappeared,

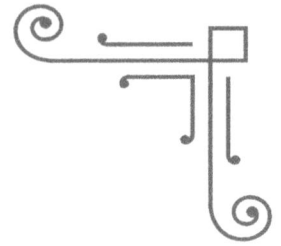

## CAVE GUARD

Mother Nature was distressed to hear,
Follow me through this large golden door.
Mother Nature is waiting to know more.

## CHORUS

And Mother Nature begins to speak.

## MOTHER NATURE

I've heard our precious butterflies wish to remain in their cocoon;
What solution do you seek and how soon?

## OSCAR the OWL

The butterflies are willing to hide.
They won't come out. They will stay inside.
They feel their cause is more than just.
No more competition. No more fuss.

## CHORUS

Bucky Beaver begins to chatter.

## BUCKY BEAVER

It's outrageous that these butterflies.
Can decide such an important matter.
We want the contest and we want the show.
Please tell the butterflies that your decision is "no".

## DELPHIA DOE

Maybe we are wrong and the butterflies are right?
Perhaps contests do create unnecessary fights.
They have a good point, why just one do we choose?
While the others must always lose?
Each butterfly is such a sweet creature.
Why is it necessary to pick only one to feature?
While taking this trip, I have had hours to spend.
Thinking about the butterflies.
And a problem that appears to have no end.
The more I think, the more it is clear.
We don't need a beauty contest on which to build fear.

## MOTHER NATURE

Delphia and the butterflies are right; we need to make amends.
Contests are for enemies; not for dear friends.
Return to the forest, and tell them what I say.
Let no more contests spoil anyone's day.
We will stop our efforts to compare.
And everyone will know we are being fair.

End the contest, there shall never again be another race.
Cherish the fact that there is uniqueness in each face.
There are differences I believe.
But you must realize each one has achieved.
Their unique beauty, each with a style of their own.
Tell the others; it is time for you to head for home.

## CHORUS

The forest friends began their journey home.
Never again would there be separation or being alone.
They came together in feeling good with the decree.
No one would be a loser; they unanimously agree.

## OSCAR the OWL

Buttercup and friends - Mother Nature has spoken loud and clear.
There won't be any more competition; none that creates fear.
and her decision has forced a way of life to end.
Now dear Butterflies, out of your cocoons you may spin.

## CHORUS

As the news travels far and wide.
The Butterflies no longer had to hide.
Buttercup was yellow and bright as gold.
She flew with a graceful flair to behold.
She danced in celebration with her friends.

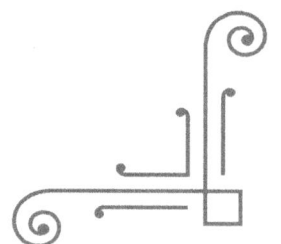

Colors of green, red and blue.

They reached the highest trees.

And touched the clouds as they flew.

The problem was gone that had plagued them all.

Now each butterfly could stand tall.

Each Spring the butterflies put on a spectacular show.

And everyone in the forest has come to know.

The real beauty is being able to see.

How the butterflies live in harmony.

For there are no losers.

Now everyone of them will win.

And this in the forest is how happiness begins.

# Buttercup and the Beauty Contest
## Competition

Buttercup the butterfly and her friends decide not to leave their cocoons because they think there is too much competition in the forest. The butterflies strike in an effort to keep the animals from competing; making one a winner and another a loser. The butterflies feel there should be a better way to get along in the forest. The animals consult with Mother Nature and a decision is made that make all the forest friends happy.

# Buttercup and the Beauty Contest
## Story Guide

1. Was Buttercup and her friends right or wrong in wanting to change the way things had been done in the forest before?

2. What do you think the butterflies meant when they said they were going to go on strike?

3. How do you think the Ferndale Forest will be without the competition? Will it be better or worse? Why?

4. Have each member of your family or group of friends say something nice about each person in the room. What are some nice things you would like to hear about you?

5. Do you think Mother Nature was right in her decision? Who suggested to Mother Nature that she make this decision? Would you have suggested a different solution? What would have been your solution?

## Reflections

6. How does your family or friends avoid competition among each other? Discuss alternative solutions so there isn't competition with your family or friends.

7. Draw your favorite butterfly using your favorite colors. Have your family or friends do the same. See if anyone tries to compare their picture with the other drawings. Have everyone describe how they feel about the comparisons.

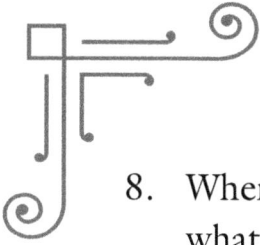

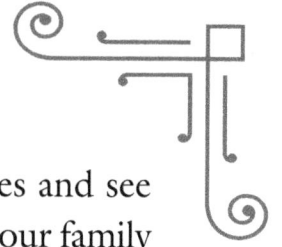

8. Where do butterflies come from? Find a book on butterflies and see what you can learn about them. Share what you learn with your family or friends. What does the word transformation mean to you? Do you want to transform your life? How would you do that?

9. Think of games that you and your family or friends can play where there are no losers. Plan to play at least one of these games once each week with your family or friends. How do you feel when you play this game compared to a game where there are winners and losers?

10. Draw or paint a picture of how you think Mother Nature looks.

# STAR

## (Theme: Identity-Purpose)

### CHORUS

It wasn't a big deal to anyone else but it was to Star. She decided she was willing to spend a lifetime to find out who and what she was. Oh, she knew she was a star but just what type of Star and why was she created? The surrounding stars begged her not to leave their galaxy.

### GROUP OF STARS

Star, little star - you could get lost out there.
To be in that big Universe where no one might care.
Why would you want to go out there all alone?
We are happy to make you comfortable in this our home.

### STAR

Thank you for your offer; it is a kind one indeed.
But it is my calling - I must honor this personal need.
I am one million, two hundred seventeen thousand years old.
I am here in the Universe - one so big; one so cold.
But I feel my calling and I need to learn why I am alive.
This journey will hopefully give me a real sense of pride.

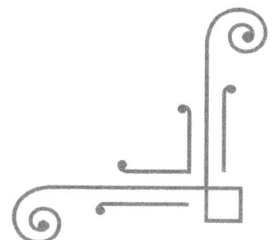

## CHORUS

With her resolve tucked firmly in her star point, she waved good-bye.
and the others waved back, each fighting back the urge to cry.
Star twirled and whirled, spinning out of sight.
She flashed all day, and throughout the night.
She was only a little thing, moving along.
She wonders if she was created to inspire a song?
Before long she saw Saturn, the planet who spoke to her.
It was wrapped with circles around and around,
The circles around Saturn were reds, yellows and browns.

## SATURN

What is your name and where do you belong?
You are so tiny not like me big and strong.
You look like a little lost star in my sky.
Do you want me to point you back home; shall I try?

## STAR

Oh no, I've come to find out who I am.
I want to know if I have any name.
I've been dreaming perhaps I have fame.
Do you know who I am, can you search your mind.
In your galaxy did I once shine?

## SATURN

Not that I know, my sweet little one.
But I'm often quite blinded by the Sun.
So, I can't help you with your search.
I hope my not knowing won't leave you in a lurch.

**STAR**

Well, I'll be on my way.
I've much to find out, so I can't stay.
I'd like to visit, but I just don't have the time.
Thanks for trying. You've been very kind.

**CHORUS**

Soon Star was spinning out of sight.
She seemed so fragile, against the darkening night.

**STAR**

Oh, you are so pretty. So bright. So rare.
I hope you don't mind if I just stare?

**SIRIUS**

Of course, little Star. I don't mind.
My name is Sirius and it happens to me all the time.
In this galaxy, I am the brightest star.
I spin, I sparkle and constantly twirl.
I bring love to young boys and girls.

**STAR**

You are lucky to know who you are.
I am just a nameless little star.
Can you tell me who I am? Have you seen me before?
Did I once live in your galaxy?
Or perhaps right next door?

## SIRIUS

That could never be.
I would certainly have remembered thee.
No, I'm sure you don't belong in this space.
You must have come from a different place.

## CHORUS

So, once again Star began to move on.
Resolving never to go back.
Until she had the name and purpose she lacked.

## STAR

Oh, this is beautiful. I know I have never seen.
So many stars with black space in between.
Do you have a name for your group?
The Northern Cross — sounds great for such a troop.
Who is the star that's at your head?
I should ask him instead.
Do you know who I am? Was I in this group?
Was I in the lower part of your loop?

## DENEB, LEADER NORTHERN CROSS

My name is Deneb and I have never seen you before.
You are not one of the stars from my little club.
But you're welcome to stay, for you we would not snub.

## STAR

If this isn't where I belong,
I should figure out how to move on.
Goodness, you are the most beautiful star in the sky.
I bet your beauty wins every heart; you don't even have to try.

## VENUS

Thank you, I am Venus and you are very sweet.
But you must be lost. Where is your own star street?

## STAR

No, until I have a name and purpose, I have no home.
But I've never seen a star with the beauty you seem to own.

## VENUS

Well, I am not really a star.
I look like one and glow like one,
but I am just a planet.
And quite different from what you are.
Stars are supposed to stay in one place.
So why are you moving around, my pretty little face?

**STAR**

You mean I am not supposed to move and twirl?
I'm supposed to be a quiet, twinkling little girl?

**VENUS**

Of course, you're breaking a major rule.
Stars stay in one place all their life.
Weren't you taught that in star school?

**STAR**

Well, maybe most stars should stay in their place.
Maybe they each know their own name and space.
But I have searched the universe everywhere.
And still have no place where someone cares.

**VENUS**

You can stay as long as you want with me.
I will watch over and care for thee.

**STAR**

No, I must be on my way.
I must complete my mission; come what may.

**CHORUS**

The Big Dipper clan stare at the little Star.

## BIG DIPPER CLAN

Well, what do we have here?
A little star coming near?
Hello, what is your name and where are you from?
Did you come from the Sun?

## STAR

Oh, I don't have a name,
And I don't know from where I came.
For many, many years I've traveled,
Past many different moons and more than one sun,
And along the way I haven't had much fun.
I feel so weary;
I feel teary.
I began my search with such hope.
All of my life I've been trying to cope.
I was sure I had some purpose, but now I'll go.
I guess there isn't anything for me to know.

## SUN

Don't give up, little one.
Look at me, I am the great Sun.
It takes millions of years to become well known.
For only over a little more than a million years have you grown.

## STAR

Are you telling me to continue my search?
Do you think I could find fortune and fame?
Do you happen to remember who I am or my name?

## SUN

No, I don't know who you are.
But I will tell you this, my brave little star.
Go find a new world if you don't have one of your own.
Don't just sit around and groan.

## STAR

Of course, you are right!

## CHORUS

Star took off to continue her flight.
She traveled further than anyone she knew.
And the longer she traveled the more tired she grew.
Darker and darker grew the sky all around,
And, of course, there wasn't any sound.

## STAR

Why is everything so dark; so black?
Perhaps I was wrong, perhaps I should turn back?
No, I will continue on my quest.
This is such an important test.
I will continue. I will succeed.
I won't stop my search until I find what I need.
I will travel until I see
Exactly the reason why I became me.

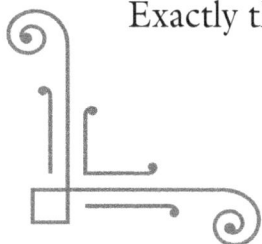

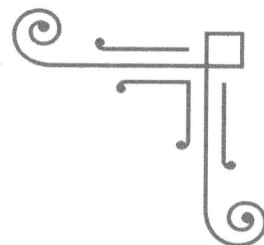

## CHORUS

Star begins to move toward the center,
Of the universe, deep in space she is about to enter.
Suddenly all the blackness becomes a bright Light.
The light is so beautiful it seems,
Like a magnificent dream.

## STAR

Why is the universe lit up this way?
It's so wonderful, I must stay.
As long as I can,
I want to be part of this Plan.

## WHITE LIGHT VOICE

My little Star, you have come so far.
What do you want? What can I do?
You have traveled a great distance.
Many miles you flew.

## STAR

Yes, I have come from far away.
If you know my fate, will you please say.
I no longer need any special fame.
Now I just want to know my own name.

## WHITE LIGHT VOICE

(soft voice sweeps over the universe)

Your story is different and you may not understand.
Do you wish to hear the unfolding of My Plan?

## STAR

Yes, I am ready, please tell me my past.
And if we have time, tell me my present and future last.

## WHITE LIGHT VOICE

You have been chosen for a specific reason.
As you know, on Earth this is the Winter season.
Your future is yet only still just a dream.
It is your present I will speak about.
So, be patient and try not to shout.
You will leave this deep part of space.
For a most unique place.

There are humans watching for your bright Light.
You will guide them by day and by night.
Once they have reached the goal that they seek.
You will watch over all while they have a chance to meet.
So, go and twirl and dance through the sky.
Don't ask questions or wonder why,
You have a reason for moving so fast.
This is a most important and valuable task.
Travel with care. You can be sure.
Your mission is great; it is very pure.

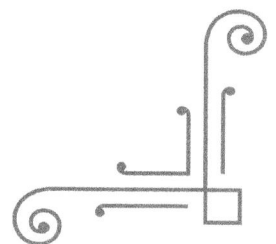

## STAR

Thank you, the brightest of Lights.
An inner voice tells me.
That where I am bound will set others free.
I will give this mission my very best.
It is the greatest of journeys -it is my quest.
My most precious Light.
My promise to you will be fulfilled.
From this point on, through Your Son's birth,
many people will be healed.
My only purpose will be to shine brighter than bright,
And it will be remembered by all on this Holy night.

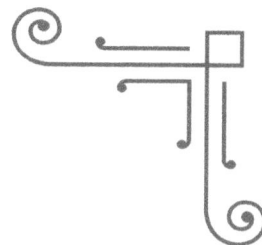

# Star

## Identity-Purpose

Star is distressed because she does not know who she is or what her purpose in life is supposed to be. Star travels throughout the solar system seeking information from the other planets and stars. Not finding any answers, she starts out toward new universes hoping to discover a solution to her problem. Ultimately, through her secret helper, star finds an identity and a purpose in life.

# Star

## Story Guide

1. Why do you think it was so important for Star to have a name and a purpose in life? Did she find out what her name was? Her purpose in life? Do you know your purpose in life? Are you fulfilling it? If not, tell a trusted friend how you could fulfill your purpose in life.

2. Name some stars and planets that were not mentioned in the story. What are some of the differences between stars and planets?

3. Name some of the planets and stars she met on her journey?

4. Who does the Light Voice represent for you?

## Reflections

5. Go to an Observatory. What is the study of astronomy? Do you think you could be interested in studying astronomy? Plan to attend a presentation about the solar system while you are at the Observatory.

6. As a group project, make a large mural of the sky putting the stars and planets in the right places and listing their names. Ask a community resource if you can hang the mural on their wall for display purposes.

7. Make costumes out of cardboard depicting various stars and planets. Then put on a family or community play using the story as a script to be performed at Christmas time, or other special occasions.

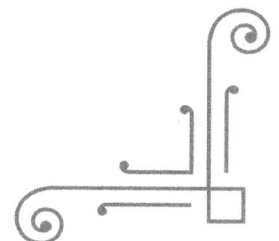

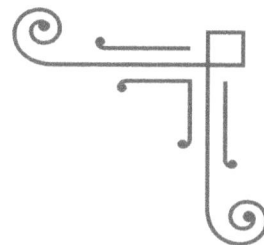

# About the Author

Jerri Curry, Ph.D., #27385 Forensic Psychologist, LMFT, #19776 Licensed Marriage and Family Therapist and CAODC #6247, Certified Alcohol and Other Drug Abuse Counselor, is also the author of the following media editorials, articles or books: California Journal (1978); Editorials for KICU TV, San Jose, CA (1979); The Swan (1988); Families in Transition, OJJDP (1989); I Believe in Angels (1995); In Search of America's Soul (2002) and One with the Light, A Mystic's Journey to the Light (2019).

She is a Forensic Clinical Psychologist who has devoted her professional life in helping the mentally ill, the homeless, those with alcohol and drug addictions, the developmentally challenged and missing and exploited children and their families. She has approached her professional life with dedication, and collective, compassionate consciousness. At the age of 75, for fifty plus years she has placed the highest priority on being a spiritual being with a social and psychological approach to solving problems for children, adults, families and citizens within the community. She continues to stay busy with a private practice in Benicia, California.

Center for Mediation and Counseling

Dr. Curry may be contacted through her website:

one-with-the-light.com

or (707) 297-0550
or write to: 77 Solano Square, #321, Benicia, CA 94510

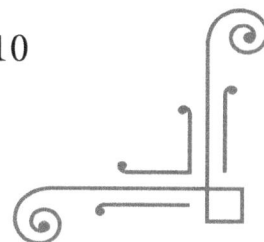

www.ingramcontent.com/pod-product-compliance
Lightning Source LLC
Chambersburg PA
CBHW041427270326
41932CB00030B/3482